THREE WISE GUYS

Scott Alan Evans
&
Jeffrey Couchman

Based on the stories
"Dancing Dan's Christmas"
and
"The Three Wise Guys"
by
Damon Runyon

BROADWAY PLAY PUBLISHING INC
New York
www.broadwayplaypub.com
info@broadwayplaypub.com

First edition: October 2018
I S B N: 978-0-88145-794-0

Book design: Marie Donovan
Page make-up: Adobe InDesign
Typeface: Palatino

THREE WISE GUYS was developed and workshopped through TACT/The Actors Company Theatre's newTACTics New Play Program & Festival in June 2017. TACT went on to present the play's World Premiere production at the Beckett Theatre/Theatre Row in New York City. It opened on 11 March 2018 with the following cast and creative contributors:

GOOD TIME CHARLEY/MYRTON/
  DOC KELTON...Ron McClary
BLONDY SWANSON...Karl Kenzler
CLARABELLE/MURIEL O'NEILL....................Victoria Mack
THE DUTCHMAN..Joel Jones
DANCING DAN..Jeffrey C Hawkins
GAMMER O'NEILL/
  MRS ALBRIGHT (BITSY)........................Dana Smith-Croll
HEINE SCHMITZ/JASPER/AMBERSHAM/
  COP..John Plumpis

Director...Scott Alan Evans
Set design...Jason Ardizzone-West
Costume design..David Toser
Lighting design...................................Mary Louise Geiger
Sound design...Bart Fasbender
Projection design..Dan Scully
Original music..Joseph Trapanese
Puppetry design...Andy Gaukel
Associate Set design.......................................Jacob Brown
Props design..Cody Lee
Wig design..................................Robert-Charles Vallance
Production stage manager...................................Kelly Burns

CHARACTERS & SETTING

Actor #1:
GOOD TIME CHARLEY BERNSTEIN, *around 50. A bartender and everybody's friend.*
MYRTON, *50s. An English butler.*
DOC KELTON, *50s. A warm-hearted, no-nonsense country doctor.*

Actor #2:
BLONDY SWANSON, *40s. Tall, burly and blond. A shrewd bootlegger with a melancholy, romantic soul.*

Actor #3:
MISS CLARABELLE COBB, *30s. Sweet and sensible former chorus girl from a religious family in Akron, Ohio.*
MURIEL O'NEILL, *30s. A beauty and deeply loyal. A trained dancer working at the Half Moon Club. A native New Yorker and a real artiste.*

Actor #4:
THE DUTCHMAN, *50s. Short, stocky, capable older guy, somewhat worn down by life.*

Actor #5:
DANCING DAN, *30s. A good-looking young guy with an easy charm. Always well dressed. Men enjoy his good humor and companionship. Women love everything about him. Originally from San Francisco.*

Actor #6:
MRS ELIZABETH ALBRIGHT (BITSY), *late 40s. An attractive and imperious society woman.*

GAMMER O'NEILL, MURIEL's *grandmother, 90-odd, and a little childish in spots.*

Actor #7:
HEINE SCHMITZ, *late 40s. Runs an extensive bootlegging and racketeering operation. Something of a powder keg.*
JASPER, *late 50s.* MYRTON's *very proper elder brother. A butler.*
AMBERSHAM, *late 40s. An officious, unctuous factory foreman.*
COP, *40s.*

Time: Christmas Eve, 1932

Streets and a speakeasy in the West forties of Manhattan.

A car on the road to Great Neck, Long Island.

The den/sitting room of a mansion in Great Neck, Long Island.

A car on the roads of Pennsylvania.

A barn in Pennsylvania.

Note: The play is designed to be presented in a highly theatrical, transformative style. The physical production should be suggested—not literal—with each location transforming simply and seamlessly from one to another.

The play is performed without intermission.

To Fiona,
and to the memory of
William R Evans, Jr

and

To Barbara and Ella

(*Darkness. We hear sounds of the city on a December day: the hum of traffic, the ringing of silver bells, and ad-lib voices calling as they move away from each other— "Merry Christmas! See you next week. Happy Holidays!....")*

(*From the darkness there emerges a single tiny star. As the hovering star grows larger and larger, it transforms into the distinct shape of a diamond. Around the glinting diamond, elegant lettering begins to appear, and the diamond is revealed to be the "O" in the words "SHAPIRO'S FINE JEWELRY", which form above a silhouette of the establishment's front door.)*

(*The door opens, and the silhouette of a man, clutching a small bundle, slips out of the jewelry store and darts away into the shadows.)*

(*CLANG CLANG CLANG! The store alarm goes off. The silhouettes of sales clerks run out of the door, looking to see in which direction the thief ran off. As the letters of the store name break into shimmering fragments, running footsteps pound the pavement and ad-lib voices converge from various directions, shouting in overlapping commotion: "What happened? It's Shapiro's! It's been robbed! Did you see it? Did they get him?..." Police sirens wail.)*

(*The glittering letters and the noises fade, and lights reveal the speakeasy of* GOOD TIME CHARLEY BERNSTEIN. *It is a no-frills joint, but it has all you need for comfort and a good time: a clean bar and a few tables.)*

(*In a nod to the season,* CHARLEY *has strung colored lights along the bar. Perhaps a scraggly Christmas tree, hung with a few sad ornaments, sits in a corner.)*

(CHARLEY *is alone in the place, straightening a chair or two.
He hums a tune that is a bewildering mash-up of "Hark! The
Herald Angels Sing" and "Hava Nagila.")*

(The song is interrupted by a rhythmic knock at the door.)

(CHARLEY *looks through the peephole and opens the door to
let in the tall and burly* BLONDY SWANSON.*)*

BLONDY: Hello, Charley.

CHARLEY: Right on time.

BLONDY: By my watch, five minutes late. But I stop to
talk with The Dutchman.

CHARLEY: I hear he has been in Chicago.

BLONDY: Well, then the Windy City blows him no
good. What he needs at this moment is hot Tom and
Jerry.

CHARLEY: This is all anyone needs.

BLONDY: Of course, two Gs would also help.

(CHARLEY moves to the bar.)

CHARLEY: Have a seat. Tom is ready and waiting for
Jerry.

(BLONDY goes over to a table near the bar and sits.)

(Meanwhile, CHARLEY *produces a punch bowl filled with
liquid from behind the bar. As he and* BLONDY *talk, he
carefully pours in cognac and rum, then stirs the mixture to
create a foaming masterpiece.)*

CHARLEY: My heart goes out to all and sundry who fall
on hard days. But I am a most fortunate man. This has
been a busy season. I hope and trust that business is
thriving with you, Blondy.

BLONDY: I have no business. I retire from business.

(CHARLEY nearly drops a bottle.)

CHARLEY: If J Pierpont Morgan or John D Rockefeller step up and tell me they retire from business, I will not be more astonished. Thousands of citizens depend on Blondy Swanson for their merchandise. Why do you get this notion?

BLONDY: Well, I retire from business because I consider myself one hundred per cent American citizen. In fact, I am a patriot. One year I even pay an income tax.

CHARLEY: Then as a patriot, it is your duty to serve the thirsty people of this great but exceedingly dry nation. *(He carries the drinks over to* BLONDY.*)*

BLONDY: I am a bootie for a long time, but I can see into the future and I can see that one of these days they are going to repeal this prohibition law. And then it will be most unpatriotic to bring in wet goods from foreign parts. So I retire.

CHARLEY: Well, Blondy, your sentiments certainly do you credit. *(Lifts his glass to* BLONDY*)* If we have more citizens as high minded as you are, this will be a better country.

BLONDY: Furthermore, Charley, there is no money in booting anymore. All the booties in this country are broke. I am broke myself.

CHARLEY: It is hard times.

BLONDY: I just lose the last piece of property I own in this world, which is the twenty-five G home I build in Atlantic City, figuring to spend the rest of my days there with Miss Clarabelle Cobb.

CHARLEY: I always consider Miss Clarabelle Cobb a most pleasant doll. Even if she does take a run-out powder on you.

BLONDY: If I only listen to Miss Clarabelle Cobb six years ago.

CHARLEY: Christmas Eve…I watch you read the letter right here at this very table.

BLONDY: Six years ago this night…

(Lights shift to illuminate the ethereal vision of a young attractive woman, MISS CLARABELLE COBB. She appears to be on a bus and has been crying.)

CLARABELLE: Dear Blondy,
By the time you read this, I will be on a bus back to Akron, Ohio. I still love you. But though you have said again and again that you will get out of the rum business, you never keep your promise. I can now only think that you care more for your business than you do for me. I will marry you if you are out of the rum business and do not have a dime, but I can never marry you as long as you are dealing in the demon rum. It is not good. It is not nice. Besides, it is illegal. I will spend this Christmas and the years to come in the bosom of my loving family. I am sick and tired for Broadway anyhow. It was fun while it lasted. Sure, it was glamorous dancing in Mr Georgie White's Scandals, and I met many wonderful girls, but the glamour is no more, and it is time for me to go home. Some day when you are really through with the terrible traffic you are engaged in, come to me.
Your ever-loving,
Clarabelle

(Lights fade on CLARABELLE.)

CHARLEY: A most pleasant doll. Now that you retire, perhaps you and Miss Clarabelle Cobb can get back together.

BLONDY: I hear she marries some legitimate guy in Akron, Ohio.

(A familiar rhythmic knock sounds at the door. CHARLEY goes to answer it.)

CHARLEY: Still, I say it is a false lie about "the demon rum," because you never handle a drop of rum in your life, but only Scotch. *(Looks through the peephole)* Santa Claus wants in.

BLONDY: That is The Dutchman. He makes a few potatoes pretending to be a jolly Santa.

(CHARLEY opens the door, and THE DUTCHMAN, short and stocky, somewhat lost in an ill-fitting Santa suit, storms in. He is wearing a large sign on his back that reads:
MOE LEWINSKY'S APPAREL
A GOOD FIT
AT A FITTING PRICE
249 W 44)

THE DUTCHMAN: Three more times! Not once. *Three* more times I have to walk around the block.

CHARLEY: Hello, Dutchman.

THE DUTCHMAN: I am done with this Santa Claus racket. It is strictly for suckers. *(He yanks off his Santa hat, wig, and beard and throws them on the bar.)*

CHARLEY: Since when are you touting for Moe Lewinsky?

THE DUTCHMAN: Since Lightning Streak does me no good in the third at Aqueduct, and Little Gringo calls in my marker. For two Gs.

CHARLEY: This is sad news.

BLONDY: Yes, Little Gringo is most impatient when it comes to markers.

THE DUTCHMAN: He is generous with me, because it is Christmastime. He gives me until tomorrow.

CHARLEY: You could use a hot Tom and Jerry.

THE DUTCHMAN: What Moe pays me does not even put a small dent in my marker. How do people work for a living?

BLONDY: You know, Charley, if I only listen to Miss Clarabelle Cobb, I will now be an honest clerk in a gents' furnishing store....

THE DUTCHMAN: I am ready to take plenty of outdoors on this old burg. Get down to sunny Florida....

BLONDY: Maybe we'd have a cute little apartment up around 110th Street and kiddies running all around and about....

THE DUTCHMAN: But that does not mean some prank like the one at Shapiro's Fine Jewelry. I have felt plenty of that heat. I am too old for heat.

(CHARLEY hands THE DUTCHMAN a glass.)

CHARLEY: To the end of heat.

(They drink.)

(Once again: the rhythmic knock at the door. As CHARLEY crosses the room, the knock is followed by the slap-shuffle-slap of tap-dancing feet.)

CHARLEY: I do not even have to look.

(CHARLEY throws open the door, and DANCING DAN breezes in. He is a trim, good-looking young man, who moves with an easy grace. He is holding a package—something wrapped in butcher paper—under his arm.)

CHARLEY: Dancing Dan!

DANCING DAN: Merry Christmas to you, Good Time Charley!

CHARLEY: *(Pointing at DANCING DAN's package)* A little something for the holiday?

DANCING DAN: A little something for Miss Muriel O'Neill.

BLONDY: You are still seeing her?

DANCING DAN: Every dance I can get.

BLONDY: Does Heine Schmitz know this? I hear he has his eye on Miss Muriel O'Neill. And Heine Schmitz is not such a guy as will take kindly to anybody dancing more than once and a half with a doll he has his eye on.

DANCING DAN: Ha Ha. Heine Schmitz has plenty of other dolls he can ogle—not to mention the wife.

BLONDY: All I can say, Dancing Dan, is you are a very brave man.

CHARLEY: And here is hot Tom and Jerry to boost your courage.

DANCING DAN: The Dutchman! I hear you are in Florida.

THE DUTCHMAN: Trying to get there, Dancing Dan. Trying to get there.

DANCING DAN: *(To* CHARLEY*)* Am I in time for the reciting of the letter?

CHARLEY: Miss Clarabelle Cobb has come and gone.

DANCING DAN: Well, there is always next Christmas Eve.

*(*CHARLEY *hands a Tom and Jerry to* DANCING DAN.*)*

DANCING DAN: Christmas in a glass. Here's to the happiest of seasons!

BLONDY: You are always the most carefree guy I know, what with your dancing around all the night and day. I wish I had such a carefree life.

DANCING DAN: It is all in how you approach things.

BLONDY: I hear you have a most interesting approach.

DANCING DAN: I have not been collared yet! *(To* THE DUTCHMAN*)* Dutchman, that is a handsome Santa Claus suit.

THE DUTCHMAN: It is hot, and it does not fit.

DANCING DAN: Yes, I would say it is more my size.…
You know, I always think I would make a good Santa
Claus—one of those jolly St. Nicks that hands out gifts
at an orphanage or an old dolls' home.

THE DUTCHMAN: You can have it.

DANCING DAN: Ho Ho Ho…

THE DUTCHMAN: No, I am serious. *(He begins pulling off
the costume, which he is wearing over his street clothes.)*

DANCING DAN: I cannot take your Santa suit.

THE DUTCHMAN: It is not *my* Santa suit. Take it!

DANCING DAN: You are sure?

THE DUTCHMAN: You can have no idea how sure I am.

DANCING DAN: This is a kind gesture, Dutchman,
but…

*(THE DUTCHMAN shoves the pieces of the suit at DANCING
DAN.)*

THE DUTCHMAN: I insist.

DANCING DAN: Alright. If you say so. Thank you. I am
curious to try it on.

THE DUTCHMAN: Knock yourself out. Just get it back to
Moe Lewinsky. And make sure it has fleas.

*(While the men continue talking, DANCING DAN puts on
the Santa costume piece by piece.)*

CHARLEY: I always wonder about Santa Claus. The
breaking and entering.

BLONDY: No, he slides down a chimbley.

DANCING DAN: Into the peaceful homes of sleeping
citizens.

CHARLEY: He sounds like a second-story man.

THE DUTCHMAN: I for one am done with Santa Claus!

BLONDY: He does not take any items from the sleeping citizens. He stuffs their stockings with goodies.

CHARLEY: This is a clever front.

DANCING DAN: Do not let Miss Muriel O'Neill's grandmamma hear you say these things.

THE DUTCHMAN: Gammer O'Neill? I am surprised to hear this old dame is still kicking.

(DANCING DAN *uses the wrapped package he brought in with him to make a round belly under his Santa jacket.*)

DANCING DAN: Gammer O'Neill is going on ninety-odd.

THE DUTCHMAN: Ninety-odd, that's something.

(*A vision of sweet, elderly* GAMMER O'NEILL *appears. She is hanging up a Christmas stocking on a bedside chair.*)

DANCING DAN: But she cannot hold out much longer, what with one thing and another, including being a little childish in spots.

(GAMMER O'NEILL *sets out a glass of milk and a small plate of cookies for Santa.*)

DANCING DAN: Miss Muriel O'Neill tells me how her Gammer hangs up her stocking on Christmas Eve all her life and always believes Santa Claus will come along some Christmas and fill the stocking full of beautiful gifts.

BLONDY: Does Santa Claus never deliver?

(*The milk and cookies being set,* GAMMER O'NEILL *sits patiently and waits for Santa.*)

DANCING DAN: He never does, though every year Miss Muriel O'Neill personally takes a few gifts home and pops them into the stocking to make Gammer O'Neill feel better.

(*The vision of* GAMMER O'NEILL *fades.*)

CHARLEY: I always say Miss Muriel O'Neill is a most pleasant doll.

(DANCING DAN *reveals himself in full Santa regalia.*)

DANCING DAN: How do I look?

CHARLEY: You are ready for your first break-in.

THE DUTCHMAN: You look more like Santa Claus than Santa Claus. How's about some holiday music? Who knows a Christmas carol?

BLONDY: I thought you are done with Santa Claus.

THE DUTCHMAN: He can go jump in the lake. Not you, Dancing Dan. The real guy. But I like music.

CHARLEY: *(Rumbling off-key)* "Hava, nagila…hava, nagila…"

THE DUTCHMAN: This is not a Christmas song.

BLONDY: Here is one Miss Clarabelle Cobb always enjoys… *(Singing)* "Will you love me in December as you do in May?…"

THE DUTCHMAN: Yes, that is a good old carol.

BLONDY & THE DUTCHMAN: *(Singing)* "Will you love me in the good old-fashioned way?…"

(DANCING DAN *and* CHARLEY *join in. They attempt barbershop-quartet harmony. They're not bad.*)

ALL:
"When my hair has all turned gray,
Will you kiss me then and say,
That you love me in December as you do in May?
(Big finish)
That you love me…

(A knock at the door)

ALL:
…in December…

(A louder knock)

ALL:
…as you do…in…May?"

(A pounding at the door!)

(CHARLEY heads for the door, while THE DUTCHMAN and BLONDY congratulate each other on their singing, and DANCING DAN goes into an elegant soft-shoe as a kind of encore.)

(CHARLEY looks out the peephole. Then he speaks in a low, warning voice.)

CHARLEY: Heine Schmitz.

(Dead silence)

(DANCING DAN, in his Santa Claus costume, pulls up the Santa beard to cover his face and moves off to a corner.)

(THE DUTCHMAN and BLONDY stand side by side, braced for trouble.)

(CHARLEY opens the door.)

(In walks HEINE SCHMITZ, compact, controlled, wearing a heavy coat and expensive leather gloves.)

CHARLEY: Heine Schmitz! The last time I see you is at Big Brandy's funeral. Merry Christmas.

(HEINE's cold gaze seems to bore right through CHARLEY.)

HEINE: Personally, I consider Christmas an overrated holiday. *(Turns his gaze on the others)* Any party that says otherwise can come speak to me.

THE DUTCHMAN: You will get no argument from me, Heine.

HEINE: The Dutchman. I hear you was in college down South.

THE DUTCHMAN: Well, I am here now.

(HEINE walks over to the bar and looks behind it.)

CHARLEY: What is your pleasure, Heine? I am serving hot Tom and Jerry for this festive—for no reason at all, if you like to join us in a glass…of something. *(He sets a glass down on the bar.)*

(HEINE picks up the glass. He barely flicks his wrist, and the glass flies out of his hand and hits the wall with an unnerving crash.)

(Silence)

BLONDY: What brings you to the West Side, Heine?

HEINE: You will find this an interesting story. I am in the neighborhood to visit my brother-in-law and to throw some business his way, because I am in the market for a little bangle. My brother-in-law is Joseph Ṣhapiro. Of Shapiro's Fine Jewelry.

BLONDY: I once buy a ring there myself. A very fine establishment.

HEINE: You always have good taste, Blondy. There is an unfortunate occurrence at Shapiro's store today. An unknown individual enters illegally upon the premises and knocks the joint off.

BLONDY: This is sad news indeed.

HEINE: Yes, very sad news. I must now find another establishment where to make my purchase. But I figure, as I am in the neighborhood, I think to look up an old acquaintance or two. I come here in the hope I see Dancing Dan. I have a proposition of great interest for him. Do any of you know where I will find Dancing Dan?

(BLONDY, THE DUTCHMAN, and CHARLEY shake their heads.)

CHARLEY: I do not see him all day.

BLONDY: No. I am busy showing my cousin from Sweden around town. *(He gestures to DANCING DAN in his Santa costume.) He* does not speak English, but he is an old hand at playing Saint Nick back home. We are on our way to hand out gifts at an old dolls' home. He is not right in the noggin. A sad story.

HEINE: Yeah, well, I am most eager to talk with Dancing Dan.

BLONDY: I have not heard of Dancing Dan for quite sometime.

THE DUTCHMAN: He is probably off on a Christmas holiday with Miss M... *(He stops himself.)*

HEINE: With who?

THE DUTCHMAN: I don't know.

HEINE: Miss Muriel O'Neill? You think Miss Muriel O'Neill would go on a Christmas holiday with Dancing Dan? Do you?

THE DUTCHMAN: What do I know, Heine?

HEINE: That's right. What do you know? Miss Muriel O'Neill has better things to do. And better people than Dancing Dan with whom to do them with. Do you understand me? Besides, she works this afternoon at the Half Moon Club. How do I know this? Because I already go to the club and speak with her. She does not see Dancing Dan all day either. But I will find him. And when I do... *(Surveys the group one last time)* Enjoy your hot Tom and Jer'. *(He strolls out the door.)*

(CHARLEY, BLONDY, and THE DUTCHMAN simultaneously look at DANCING DAN.)

DANCING DAN: Say, Charley, how about another one of these delicious hot Tom and Jer's?

CHARLEY: Whatever you say, Dancing Dan.

DANCING DAN: Anyone for another song?

(No takers. The guys drink in silence. Then...)

THE DUTCHMAN: You know, my old can is parked on Fifty-third Street. A nice drive might be just the thing on a fine night like this.

DANCING DAN: A car ride can be most pleasant.

BLONDY: I remember you have an uncle lives in New Brunswick.

THE DUTCHMAN: I am with him not so long ago. But to tell you the truth, my uncle makes it clear that I overstay my welcome. So New Brunswick is out.

BLONDY: Ah…

THE DUTCHMAN: But I do know a place over in Pennsylvania. I have been thinking of going back there myself.

DANCING DAN: I never see Pennsylvania. I hear it is fine open country.

THE DUTCHMAN: With many scenic views.

DANCING DAN: Yes…a nice drive on a fine night could be just the thing.

THE DUTCHMAN: So, what do you say?

DANCING DAN: Why not? Blondy, you are welcome to join us.

THE DUTCHMAN: That's right, Blondy, you will want to walk out with your cousin from Sweden, in case anyone cares to watch Good Time Charley's door.

BLONDY: If I stay here or take a ride, it is still the same old Christmas Eve.

(CHARLEY *serves up another round of hot Tom and Jerry.*)

CHARLEY: One for the road, gentlemen. Merry Christmas to all.

(*At the same time:*)

DANCING DAN: Merry Christmas!

BLONDY: So you say.

THE DUTCHMAN: To the road ahead.

(They down their drinks.)

DANCING DAN: This is my party tonight, Charley. I will settle up with you in the New Year.

CHARLEY: I know you will be good for it, Dancing Dan.

THE DUTCHMAN: Next time, it is on me.

BLONDY: Good Time Charley, why do you not close up the joint and come with us? You are always good company.

CHARLEY: I wish I could. But tonight of all nights I must keep the doors open and provide what holiday comfort I can to those in need. It is sure to be one of the biggest regrets in my life that I am unable to accompany you on this adventure. At least let me send you off with a little Tom and Jerry for your merry jaunt. *(He hands BLONDY a glass jar full of Tom and Jerry.)*

DANCING DAN: This is most kind of you, Charley.

BLONDY: Yes, thank you.

THE DUTCHMAN: Gentleman, shall we?

(THE DUTCHMAN heads to the door, followed by BLONDY and DANCING DAN.)

DANCING DAN: I have a small package to deliver before we head to P A. It will not take long.

(They go.)

(CHARLEY locks the door behind them and goes back to work.)

(Lights)

(DANCING DAN in the Santa Claus suit, THE DUTCHMAN, and BLONDY are on Fifty-third Street, staring at an empty parking space.)

DANCING DAN: You are sure?

THE DUTCHMAN: Yes, this is right where I parked it! It was an old can. Who would want it?

(They stand there for a moment in thought.)

THE DUTCHMAN: I am wondering…Santa Claus can break into citizens' houses on Christmas Eve.

BLONDY: He does not break in.

THE DUTCHMAN: Well, he is allowed to go in through the chimney. I am thinking it is also on the up and up for Santa to take any automobile he happens to find unoccupied on Christmas Eve.

BLONDY: It will be hard to convince a judge.

(BLONDY is taking a swig from the jar of Tom and Jerry when suddenly from offstage a voice with a British accent calls out.)

MYRTON: *(Off)* I say! …Hello there! Hello! …Excuse me!

(MYRTON appears and runs frantically up to the three guys. He is wearing a butler's uniform and lugging four large shopping bags stuffed with toys and rolls of Christmas paper.)

MYRTON: Thank goodness I've found you! Providence. Pure providence. My Santa. At last!

DANCING DAN: Set this to music, friend.

(The guys start to walk away.)

MYRTON: No, no, please! …Wait. I must have a Santa. I need a Santa. The situation is really quite dire. *(He grabs on to DANCING DAN.)*

BLONDY: Easy there, fella.

MYRTON: No. Wait. You don't understand. I will hire you. I wish to *hire* you. To be Santa. You see?

DANCING DAN: Thanks, buddy, but we got other plans…

MYRTON: Oh, no, no, no, no, no. I will double whatever you have been offered. I—I—I will treble it! My employer…Mrs Albright…will treble it.

THE DUTCHMAN: Albright? Of the Long Island Albrights?

MYRTON: Oh, you know her?

THE DUTCHMAN: I know *of* her.

MYRTON: Ah, well, yes…you see, tonight is her annual Christmas party.

THE DUTCHMAN: At the place in Great Neck?

MYRTON: Yes, in Great Neck. Yes. Precisely! This party is the pinnacle of the social season in Great Neck—no, let us say all of Long Island. It will be attended by the most powerful and influential of the elite.

BLONDY: Studs Doogan?

MYRTON: Um…perhaps…yes, I have no doubt Mr Doogan will be in attendance. And this year, out of the goodness of her heart, Mrs Albright has invited young people from the Whitley School for Wayward Boys, for whom she is intent on bestowing a bit of Christmas cheer. So you see how important you are. I mean Santa. We can't let the boys down. No, no, we simply can't. But we must leave now. The party begins…Oh, my! Within the hour!

DANCING DAN: Hold on a minute there, Jeeves. How does it come about that such a swell holiday bash is planned with no Santa Claus for the little children?

MYRTON: Oh, Santa was planned. I hired him myself. Forgive me, my name is Myrton. I hired a friend of mine…Rufus Holloway. I went so far as to give him money to buy gifts for the unfortunate boys. But the

fellow betrayed me. He lost most of the money on a
racing track bet.

THE DUTCHMAN: This is not an uncommon situation.

MYRTON: Yes, but then he drank up what was left.
I cannot in good conscience have a drunken Santa
around impressionable children.

BLONDY: No, this sets a bad example and does harm to
the reputation of Santa Claus.

MYRTON: And what is worse, my former friend lost the
money while betting on a hunch. A hunch! How could
one ever bet on a hunch?

DANCING DAN: I have a hunch he is not the first.

THE DUTCHMAN: Do you have a system for the ponies?

MYRTON: Quite an infallible one, actually. Are you
interested in the equestrian arts?

THE DUTCHMAN: I have been known to wager a buck
or two in the past, if that's what you mean.

MYRTON: Well, I would be more than delighted to
share any and all knowledge about my system with
you...*after* the party. Time is of the essence. Please,
gentlemen. Mrs Albright knows nothing of all these
little difficulties. She is unaware that I slipped out to
buy these gifts—and to find a Santa Claus. I have been
in and out of every department store in the city *and* the
Salvation Army. *(To* DANCING DAN*)* You, I fear, are my
last hope.

THE DUTCHMAN: Give us a minute.

*(*THE DUTCHMAN, DANCING DAN, *and* BLONDY *step aside
to confer.)*

THE DUTCHMAN: He seems like a right gee.

DANCING DAN: How is it you know about these
Albrights and their house?

THE DUTCHMAN: In my younger days I am acquainted with some of the swankier homes on Long Island, on account of I make quite a good thing of knocking off safes in these swanky homes. This Albright guy makes a killing in corsets or something. And his wife is no slouch either. They say her family come over on the Mayflower. She knows many influential citizens. Her friend Judge Thrasher once gives me a year's stretch in the sneezer.

BLONDY: *(To* DANCING DAN*)* You can make a few good bobs at this brawl.

THE DUTCHMAN: Sure, but money will only give you carfare back to Manhattan, and Manhattan is where you do not want to be back to. What we need right now is a car. We gotta get to P A. We gotta.

*(*DANCING DAN *considers this and turns back to* MYRTON.*)*

DANCING DAN: I am your Santa Claus.

MYRTON: Thank goodness!

DANCING DAN: With the following conditions…

MYRTON: Oh.

DANCING DAN: First, Blondy Swanson and The Dutchman here are my elves.

MYRTON: Elves?

DANCING DAN: Santa has elves. This is common knowledge. They are part of the package.

MYRTON: Fine. Bring the elves. The more the merrier, I say.

DANCING DAN: Second, in payment, we want to borrow a car.

MYRTON: A car?

DANCING DAN: Yes, a car. For a day. Maybe three. A week tops. Nothing fancy—any car will do.

MYRTON: All right, all right. As you wish. I will get you a car. Do we have a deal?

DANCING DAN: It is a deal. Lead the way, Myrton.

MYRTON: Oh, thank you, thank you. You won't regret it, I assure you. (*Grabs his bags and bustles forward*) This way. The car is parked just around the corner.

DANCING DAN: Oh, I have one quick errand to run before—

MYRTON: Oh, no! Quite impossible. We have no time. No time! (*And he's off.*)

BLONDY: I guess we run no errands.

(*The three guys hurry along behind.*)

(*Lights*)

(MYRTON *is in the driver's seat of a Buick Town Car as he drives at what seems to be breakneck speed.* THE DUTCHMAN *is sitting shotgun;* DANCING DAN *and* BLONDY *are in the back. The three guys are hastily wrapping the Christmas presents from Myrton's bags. Wrapped presents are piled up. Paper and empty rolls are strewn all over the car.*)

THE DUTCHMAN: How many more presents we got?

BLONDY: Plenty. Looks like he buys out Macy's.

DANCING DAN: You know, Myrton, when I buy Miss Muriel O'Neill a trinket here and there, I always have the store wrap the item. Hand me the tape, Blondy.

MYRTON: On Christmas Eve, the lines for gift wrapping stretch out the door. Swiftly, gentlemen, we are in the home stretch.

BLONDY: (*To* THE DUTCHMAN) Pass me the paper with the snowmen.

(THE DUTCHMAN *passes the paper to the back seat.*)

DANCING DAN: *(To* BLONDY*)* How about some more of that Tom and Jerry?

BLONDY: Both Tom and Jerry make their departure about twenty miles ago.

(The guys continue to wrap the presents.)

THE DUTCHMAN: This is a nice car. Is this your car, Myrton?

MYRTON: This was one of Mr Albright's.

THE DUTCHMAN: Was? Is Mr Albright no longer with us?

MYRTON: Well, he is no longer with Mrs Albright.

BLONDY: Does he take a run-out powder on her?

MYRTON: No, actually, she became impatient with his extramarital activities, and she sent him packing.

BLONDY: Oh.

THE DUTCHMAN: Still, it is a nice car.

*(*MYRTON *looks into his rearview mirror.)*

MYRTON: Dan—forgive me…*Dancing* Dan—may I suggest folding the edges of the paper before taping them down?

DANCING DAN: This is the new modern style of wrapping, Myrton. I am what Miss Muriel O'Neill calls a "trendsetter."

MYRTON: Yes, well, might you try…

*(*MYRTON *reaches around behind him to help* DANCING DAN. *The car swerves.* THE DUTCHMAN *grabs the wheel as a passing car horn blares.)*

THE DUTCHMAN: Whoa! Let's keep our eyes on the road there!

MYRTON: I will take the instruction to heart.

*(*MYRTON *drives. The guys wrap gifts.)*

THE DUTCHMAN: So, Myrton, you're not from around here, are you?

MYRTON: Oh, no, Mr The Dutchman, I am a reluctant transplant from Great Britain.

THE DUTCHMAN: A long way from home.

MYRTON: Indeed.

THE DUTCHMAN: How long you been in the U S of A?

MYRTON: Just a few months actually.

THE DUTCHMAN: And you land such a good job so fast!

MYRTON: Well, my brother arranged it…in his way.

THE DUTCHMAN: I got three brothers. They once arrange to get me out of the slammer.

MYRTON: Well, my brother was living here and he suggested I come to America. You see, things were a bit complicated for me at the time back home, and I wrote to my brother for, um, advice….

(MYRTON's *very proper elder brother,* JASPER, *appears.*)

JASPER: No, Myrton, I will not send you any more money. I am dismayed to hear yet again that matters have become so desperate for you. How can you be so irresponsible? Gambling. Really! It won't do. I have secured you a position here on Long Island at the home where I am employed. You will give up the foolish life you have been leading and return to the honorable profession that our family has followed for generations: Service. Need I remind you, your great, great, great, great grandfa—

MYRTON: We are approaching the house. (*He turns the car sharply into the long driveway.*)

(*Lights out on* JASPER.)

(*At the same time:*)

DANCING DAN: So soon?

THE DUTCHMAN: You really clipped along!

BLONDY: But wait a minute, wait a minute…we are not yet done with the wrapping.

MYRTON: We must finish inside. Pack everything up!

(The guys gather up the presents and wrapping paraphernalia.)

BLONDY: Where are the scissors?

DANCING DAN: Okay, hang on there…give me a minute.

THE DUTCHMAN: You want all this stuff in the house?

MYRTON: Yes, of course, it all must come in.

BLONDY: Where are the scissors?

DANCING DAN & THE DUTCHMAN: I don't know!

(MYRTON stops the car with a jolt.)

MYRTON: Time, gentlemen, time. Madam is sure to be wondering where I've been. Come, come, come…to the party!

(Lights)

(A luxurious den of the Albright mansion, Great Neck, Long Island)

(From a distant room, we hear the festive sounds of a party: a murmur of voices, laughter, and the upbeat rhythms of a jazzy trio.)

(A door flings open, and MYRTON rushes in, followed by BLONDY, THE DUTCHMAN, and DANCING DAN in his Santa costume, each carrying an armful of wrapped [and one or two unwrapped] presents.)

MYRTON: This way. Quickly, quickly!

DANCING DAN: *(Indicating the music)* Say, Myrton. That sounds a lot like Kip Knudson. *(Even with packages in hand, he manages a few nimble steps across the floor.)*

MYRTON: Indeed, yes, that is Mr Knudson and his trio. They are entertaining during the cocktail hour.

DANCING DAN: You hear that, Blondy? Kip Knudson!

BLONDY: *(Unimpressed)* I hear. Some shindig.

(MYRTON shoves the door closed. The sound of the trio cuts out.)

MYRTON: Gentlemen, please! There are still presents to wrap, we need Santa on the job, we are far behind schedule…

(Another door swings open, and the doorway fills with the imposing figure of MRS ELIZABETH [BITSY] ALBRIGHT. Attractive, patrician, and not to be trifled with, she does not look pleased.)

BITSY: Myrton! *There* you are.

MYRTON: Good evening, Madam. I trust the party is going well.

BITSY: No, Myrton, I can't say that it is. Where have you been?

MYRTON: *(Flustered)* Ah, you see, Madam…

BITSY: The boys from the Whitley School arrived half an hour ago. They are in the library, and they are restless and waiting for Santa. I do not like restless boys in my library.

MYRTON: Nor do I, Madam.

BITSY: Did I not make it clear that you were to take care of this simple task?

MYRTON: No…that is, yes, of course…and…um…here he is. Santa. You see?

BITSY: I am not blind, Myrton.

MYRTON: And he is…you see…Madam…he is a very special Santa.

BITSY: Is he now?

MYRTON: Yes…this special Santa is…unique.

BITSY: Unique. How so?

MYRTON: Well…um…

BITSY: Yes?

DANCING DAN: You see—Mrs Albright, is it? A pleasure to make your acquaintance—I am, by all accounts, if I say so myself, one of the topmost Santa Clauses in the trade. And I must commend you on your butler here. A very resourceful fellow.

BITSY: Really?

DANCING DAN: Now I do not know how Myrton does this, but he hears that the hostess who hires me for her ritzy party in Manhattan, and who shall remain nameless, falls ill and has to cancel her blow-out at the last minute.

THE DUTCHMAN: He must have heard it through the buttle network.

DANCING DAN: Certainly, he hears it through the buttle network. And with prompt action, he is in the nick of time…

THE DUTCHMAN: Or let us say the Saint Nick of time.

DANCING DAN: …to snatch me up and "close the deal".

BITSY: *(To* MYRTON*)* You left the house and went all the way into the city?

DANCING DAN: How he makes it there and back so quick is a miracle.

MYRTON: It was the least I could do. We had to have a Santa.

BITSY: I see. *(Turns on* BLONDY *and* THE DUTCHMAN*)* And who are you?

MYRTON: These are Santa's helpers.

BITSY: His helpers?

MYRTON: His renowned Elves. I know how important these unfortunate boys are to you, and I wanted to be sure Santa has all the assistance he needs.

BITSY: So where are their costumes?

MYRTON: Their costumes?

BITSY: Yes, their elves' costumes.

BLONDY: Stolen.

BITSY: Stolen?

BLONDY: It is a sad fact that not everyone at this time of year has the proper Christmas spirit.

THE DUTCHMAN: If we catch up with the perpetrators, we will help them understand the true meaning of the season.

DANCING DAN: Mrs Albright, I am told by one and all that I cannot consider myself a true Santa Claus until I appear at your Christmas party. It is known far and wide as the party of the year, and this year more than ever, because you are helping so many unfortunate boys. It is my belief that a party such as yours is a shining light of hope for youngsters who, through no fault of their own, fall in with bad company and do things they now regret. My two associates are familiar with many such boys at many different reform schools. They do not need costumes to show these boys how to stay on the right side of the law.

MYRTON: Quite true. They are "elves" in a...a broader sense.

BITSY: I see. They are metaphoric elves.

DANCING DAN: That's it! Why, Mrs Albright, you take the words right out of my mouth. That's what they are.

These…metaphoric elves are sure to put a Christmas smile on the faces of these young boys.

BITSY: *(To* MYRTON*)* Perhaps you can find them hats of some kind.

MYRTON: No doubt, Madam.

DANCING DAN: Hats are always welcome. And if there is time later, Mrs Albright, it will be my esteemed pleasure to invite you to take a small spin around the dance floor. You should know I am the only dancing Santa on the Eastern seaboard.

BITSY: A dancing Santa?

DANCING DAN: At your service.

BITSY: I do like a fox trot.

DANCING DAN: This is my favorite.

BITSY: We shall see. *(To* MYRTON*)* The band from the Half Moon Club is setting up in the ballroom, and there is some question as to the lighting. Look into it.

MYRTON: Certainly, Madam.

BITSY: The Moonbeam girls can change on the second floor of the west wing—see they use only the back stairs—and let them know they must be quick. They perform just before dinner. Check to be certain the champagne has arrived. And, oh yes, cook cannot locate the Louisiana crayfish that were sent up for the special hors d'oeuvres for Mrs Wilberforce. Find them. Now.

MYRTON: I will attend to it all, Madam, just as soon as I introduce Santa to the boys. Everything will run smoothly, I assure you.

BITSY: It had better, Myrton. Or I'm afraid this will be the last party you ever preside over. *(She sweeps out.)*

MYRTON: Yes, Madam…

DANCING DAN: The Moonbeams! They're here? I have to go find Muriel.

(DANCING DAN *takes a step toward the door.* THE DUTCHMAN *blocks his way.*)

THE DUTCHMAN: Let us finish our job here so we can get the car we are promised—and then get to P A. That is where we want to be.

MYRTON: Excellent advice. You heard Mrs Albright. I am hanging on by the thinnest of threads.

DANCING DAN: Well...all right. I will find Muriel later. I do not want to see anyone lose their job in these times.

MYRTON: Thank you, thank you. Now quickly, let us finish up with these gifts.

(*All three guys hastily wrap the remaining presents.* MYRTON *pitches in to help.*)

DANCING DAN: (*To* BLONDY) Gimme that one.

BLONDY: No, no. Let me wrap the baseball glove.

THE DUTCHMAN: (*To* MYRTON) Can't your brother put in a good word for you here?

MYRTON: Sadly, no. Shortly after my arrival on these shores, my dear brother had a heart attack and died.

THE DUTCHMAN: That's tough.

MYRTON: Yes, it's been quite an adjustment. I inherited his position, and I fear I am not living up to Mrs Albright's high standards—nor to my brother's. But then my spirit is not in the butlerhood.

THE DUTCHMAN: What about your surefire system? With that working for you, you do not need this butling.

MYRTON: The system requires full-time attention at the track and more capital than I have at the moment.

(Noticing BLONDY's *careful wrapping)* I must say, Blondy, you are a splendid gift wrapper.

BLONDY: I learn as a young gee that a doll always appreciates a nicely wrapped present.

MYRTON: Excellent. You stay here and finish the last gift. Bring it in as soon as you are done. Santa, you and your elf come with me!

*(*DANCING DAN *and* THE DUTCHMAN *gather up the wrapped gifts.)*

THE DUTCHMAN: We are coming.

DANCING DAN: *(To* THE DUTCHMAN*)* You got it all?

THE DUTCHMAN: I got it.

MYRTON: *(To* BLONDY*)* You will find the boys in the library. The end of the corridor, on the left. *(To* DANCING DAN *and* THE DUTCHMAN*)* Follow me. *(He hurries out.)*

(On the way to the door, DANCING DAN *tries out a couple of different Santa laughs.)*

DANCING DAN: *(To* THE DUTCHMAN*)* Listen to this: Ho, ho ho. *(Lower)* Ho, ho, HO! Which do you like?

THE DUTCHMAN: They will both frighten the children.

*(*DANCING DAN *exits.)*

THE DUTCHMAN: Next year I will go somewhere that does not celebrate Christmas. *(He exits.)*

(Alone, BLONDY *swiftly wraps the final gift—perhaps a rubber hatchet.)*

(Suddenly, MISS MURIEL O'NEILL *ducks into the room. Lithe and lovely, the young woman is clearly trying to evade someone. She closes the door and listens for footsteps outside. Relieved, she turns and is dumbfounded to see* BLONDY.)*

MURIEL: Blondy Swanson!

BLONDY: Hello, Muriel. I hear you and the Moonbeams are dancing this evening. I am sorry I will not be around to see the show.

MURIEL: What is going on? Why are you both here?

BLONDY: Both?…

(HEINE *enters.*)

HEINE: Muriel. I thought I see you— *(Realizing they are not alone)* Blondy Swanson?

BLONDY: Hello, Heine. Enjoying the party? *(He scoops up his wrapped presents and heads for the door.)*

HEINE: What are you doing here? You tell me you are going to an old dolls' home.

BLONDY: Well, Mrs Albright is an old doll. *(And he is out the door.)*

MURIEL: I'm surprised to see you again so soon, Heine.

HEINE: You should have told me you were performing here tonight. I could have given you a lift from the club.

MURIEL: What a nice thought. Do you know these people?

HEINE: I hope you are not running away from me just now.

MURIEL: Oh, no, Heine. I see Blondy Swanson come in here, so I step in to say hello. But please excuse me now, I must go change.

HEINE: You have time. *(Blocks the door)*

MURIEL: Well, the show is supposed to start soon and I should make sure that the rest of the girls are—

HEINE: It is Christmas Eve, Muriel.

MURIEL: Yes. It is. December the twenty-fourth.

HEINE: This is not my favorite time of year.

MURIEL: I am sorry to hear that.

HEINE: You are always a sympathetic soul. And you know, Muriel, I have been very blue as of late.

MURIEL: Well, a New Year is just around the corner.

HEINE: My wife is in Miami, spending my money— her alimony—on trinkets such as diamond bracelets and fur coats, though why anyone needs a fur coat in Miami I do not understand.

MURIEL: Heine, I did not know you were divorced.

HEINE: Oh, we will be.

MURIEL: Still, you have your children.

HEINE: No. My children are with her in the Florida sunshine. And then they hate me anyway. My family is little comfort all around. My own sister—do you know Miss Gerta Schmitz Shapiro?

MURIEL: I have not had the pleasure.

HEINE: It is just as well. Gerta—my own sister—puts the heat on me to find out who is it that borrows merchandise from her husband's jewelry store.

MURIEL: Yes, so you said this afternoon.

HEINE: Now my sister makes me come up with a ten-thousand-dollar reward. Out of my own pocket. And no questions asked. Me? I got plenty of questions. So you see how it is, Muriel: I am a man alone. On Christmas Eve.

MURIEL: Well, I'm sure this party will cheer you up.

HEINE: I think it will take more than a party. *(Moves closer)* Besides, I am not here for the festivities. I figure to take my mind off my troubles—not to mention this suckers' day they call Christmas—I will personally make the delivery for this Albright dame.

MURIEL: Work is a good way to take your mind off things. I'm working here myself, and I should really be—

HEINE: And now I find you here, and it is like it was meant to be. Like a sign, you know? A gift. And certainly the brightest spot in a day that is a loss in anybody's books. *(Moves closer still)* Muriel, it is a rule of my life that I am always nice to anyone who is nice to me.

MURIEL: Yes, I hear it is a very healthy thing to be nice to you, Heine.

HEINE: I know you are a doll with ambitions. I can help you. I am happy to talk with you about it one night over a bottle and a bird.

MURIEL: You are always a gentleman with me, Heine. From the very first day I start at the Half Moon Club. When I meet you, I think, "There is a most distinguished older gentleman." In many ways, you make me think of my father. You have much in common with my old dad.

(A chilly silence from HEINE.)

HEINE: You know, I still have not found Dancing Dan yet.

MURIEL: No?

HEINE: No.

MURIEL: It is my guess he is spending a quiet Christmas Eve with old friends.

HEINE: He should be here with you, Muriel. This is no way to treat a beautiful doll such as you. Personally, I always treat a doll with respect.

(BITSY enters. She stops short at the sight of MURIEL and HEINE.)

BITSY: *(To MURIEL)* Who are you?

MURIEL: Muriel O'Neill.

BITSY: Aren't you one of the dancing girls?

MURIEL: Yes. I am the lead.

BITSY: Then I suggest you go lead. The show will begin soon.

MURIEL: Yes, ma'am. (*She makes a swift exit.*)

BITSY: (*To* HEINE) And who might you be?

HEINE: I am delivering the special shipment that was ordered for the evening.

BITSY: The Louisiana crayfish?

HEINE: No. This delivery is of the liquid variety.

BITSY: Oh. The champagne. Very good. Judge Thrasher tells me that his connection deals only in the highest quality.

HEINE: Our champagne is served in the courts of Europe. It satisfies kings.

BITSY: Yes, well, tonight we just have to satisfy a few senators and a lame-duck governor. Tell your boss that I will thank him in a concrete way through Judge Thrasher. I will see that you are taken care of, as well. (*Seems to take him in for the first time*) I must say, I like your manner. Your boss is lucky to have you.

HEINE: Thanks, I'll be sure to tell him.

(MYRTON *hurries in, surprised to find* BITSY *and* HEINE.)

MYRTON: Oh.

BITSY: I have been looking for you.

MYRTON: And I for you, Madam. I have checked on the delivery of tonight's beverage, and I am pleased to announce that it has arrived and has been put on ice.

BITSY: Yes, yes, I know all about the champagne. Is everything else—

MYRTON: Under control, Madam. The boys have opened their gifts and are ready to be presented to the guests.

HEINE: I see boys in the hall carrying on like a Wild West show I once take in at Madison Square Garden.

BITSY: *(Glaring at* MYRTON*)* An unfortunate occurrence. They should have been kept in the library. *(To* HEINE*)* These are youngsters from a school for juveniles in trouble. This is what you might call a pet project of mine: helping the delinquent youth of the city avoid a life of crime.

HEINE: This is a most noble enterprise. A life of crime is not what it used to be.

BITSY: Yes, these are dangerous times indeed. Now I must get back to my guests. Thank you for your service. Before you leave, you are welcome to enjoy a bite of supper in the kitchen. Myrton, show him the way. And then bring on our Santa Claus and all the boys! *(She exits.)*

HEINE: I hope Mr Albright knows how to treat a lady like that.

MYRTON: There is only a former Mr Albright.

HEINE: He croaks?

MYRTON: He is alive and as well as can be expected. Madam and Mr Albright went their separate ways about a year ago. *(He opens the door and waits for* HEINE.*)*

HEINE: A long time to be alone.

MYRTON: Mrs Albright keeps a very active social calendar. This way to the kitchen.

*(*HEINE *and* MYRTON *exit.)*

*(*BLONDY *cautiously opens the door and peers in.)*

BLONDY: He's gone.

(BLONDY *and* THE DUTCHMAN *enter, both wearing elf hats.)*

THE DUTCHMAN: Do you think Heine follows us here? Is he on to Dancing Dan?

BLONDY: No, I think maybe he follows Miss Muriel O'Neill.

THE DUTCHMAN: Dancing Dan does not need to know this.

BLONDY: We have to get him out of here. And fast.

THE DUTCHMAN: Yes, but I never see a guy who takes to the Santa business like Dancing Dan. Those boys love him.

BLONDY: Those are not boys. Those are little monsters. With sharp teeth. I tell you, Dutchman, there is one time when I almost pick up a pair of Mrs Albright's candlesticks and bop a couple of them boys on the beezer. It is a good thing you discover the eggnog.

THE DUTCHMAN: Even the boys who say they do not like eggnog like this eggnog. *(He pulls out a flask, takes a swig, and is disappointed to discover that the flask is empty.)*

BLONDY: I will grab Dancing Dan as soon as he has finished showing off the boys to the guests. And I will tell him about Heine.

THE DUTCHMAN: Good. I will find Myrton and—

(MYRTON *enters.)*

MYRTON: What are you doing in here?

THE DUTCHMAN: I am glad you come in…

MYRTON: You are not the elves I thought you were. Your place is out there with the boys. Those barbarians!

BLONDY: What do you mean? Aren't they with Santa Dan and the guests?

MYRTON: No, they are not. They are chasing each other with bows and arrows, they are shooting off cap pistols, they are playing baseball in the solarium. The solarium! And if I didn't know better, I would say some of them are drunk.

THE DUTCHMAN: *(Quickly pocketing his flask)* Boys will be boys.

MYRTON: And Santa Claus is no help. Do you know what Santa is doing? He is dancing with the guests. Dancing with the guests!

BLONDY: *(To* THE DUTCHMAN*)* This is not good.

MYRTON: What's to be done? What's to be done? Mrs Albright will be furious.

BLONDY: The thing is, Myrton, we have a small problem.

MYRTON: The problem is out there, wreaking havoc as we speak.

BLONDY: The real problem, Myrton, is that what with one thing and another, a man named Heine Schmitz is after Dancing Dan.

MYRTON: Heine Schmitz, whoever he may be…

BLONDY: Heine Schmitz is a very influential citizen of Harlem with large interests in beer and other goods.

THE DUTCHMAN: He will just as soon blow your brains out as look at you.

BLONDY: In fact, I hear sooner.

MYRTON: Nevertheless, he is of no concern to me at the moment.

BLONDY: Heine Schmitz is at this party.

MYRTON: Ah.

BLONDY: If it comes to his attention that Santa Claus is Dancing Dan, this will be a problem for one and all.

MYRTON: You make a sound point.

THE DUTCHMAN: If we blow, the party goes on without any unpleasant interruptions. So we need that car. Now.

MYRTON: The car is yours—just as soon as you bring these hooligans under control. Quid pro quo.

BLONDY: Does this mean you will not welsh on your end?

MYRTON: I am from England, sir, not from Wales!

BLONDY: Consider those boys taken care of. *(Quietly to* THE DUTCHMAN*)* Stick here and get that car. *(He heads to the door, picking up a candlestick on his way, and exits.)*

THE DUTCHMAN: Everything's going to be okay, Myrton.

MYRTON: No, no, I am not cut out for this life of service. I lived a very different life in Great Britain.

THE DUTCHMAN: Was that where you come up with your surefire system for the ponies?

MYRTON: Back home, I lived entirely off my winnings.

THE DUTCHMAN: So what happens?

MYRTON: It seemed my earnings cut into the take of Skelley O'Brien. No doubt you've heard of Mr O'Brien? "Skelley the Skull"?

THE DUTCHMAN: I get the picture. The old country was not so healthy for you.

MYRTON: And all I want in my new country is enough money to get out of this livery. I hear there is an excellent track in Yonkers.

THE DUTCHMAN: You ever hear of Hialeah?

MYRTON: Hi-a-what?

THE DUTCHMAN: That's the name of the track. Hialeah. In Florida. That's where I'm headed.

MYRTON: Are you really?

THE DUTCHMAN: Yes, down South: palm trees, oranges, and plenty of action.

MYRTON: Sounds heavenly.

THE DUTCHMAN: That's what it is. Heaven, but with better odds. I tell you what, Myrton, I bet you could use someone who knows the ropes. And I could sure use a new partner. What do you say we team up?

MYRTON: Well, that is a most surprising proposition, Mr—

THE DUTCHMAN: Just call me Dutchman.

MYRTON: ...Mr Dutchman.

THE DUTCHMAN: Okay.

MYRTON: To partner with a man of your obvious experience could be advantageous. Most advantageous. But I'm afraid I haven't the means for such a journey. I understand it costs many thousands of dollars.

THE DUTCHMAN: Who gave you that guff? We can get going with a grand.

MYRTON: A grand?

THE DUTCHMAN: A thousand bills.

MYRTON: Bills?

THE DUTCHMAN: Clams.

MYRTON: Clams?

THE DUTCHMAN: DOLLARS!

MYRTON: Ah. Why, I have nearly that much already! What with my brother's legacy and the bonus Mrs

Albright has promised me tonight, I should be well over the top.

THE DUTCHMAN: Then we're all set. I am working on an angle myself. And if all goes well in P A later, by this time tomorrow I will have more than my share too.

MYRTON: Wonderful!

THE DUTCHMAN: You said it.

MYRTON: But wait. I still have to earn that bonus. Oh, my, the boys! Come, come, come, we have work to do.

THE DUTCHMAN: I'm with you, Myrton. We will settle those boys and then get that car.

(MYRTON *and* THE DUTCHMAN *exit.*)

(*Through the other door,* DANCING DAN *in his Santa costume bursts into the room.*)

DANCING DAN: Hey, why aren't you guys?... (*He is surprised to discover the room is empty.*)

(MURIEL *enters, wearing her dancing Moonbeam costume.*)

MURIEL: Dan?...

DANCING DAN: Well, hello there... (*Grabs her and plants a loving kiss on her lips*) Mmmm...naughty *and* nice.

MURIEL: I'm so glad you're safe. (*Indicating his Santa suit*) But what are you doing here?

DANCING DAN: Having a swell time!

MURIEL: Do you know that Heine Schmitz is at the party?

(DANCING DAN *takes hold of* MURIEL *and dances her across the floor.*)

DANCING DAN: Sure. I hope he enjoys himself. Heine Schmitz does not worry me.

MURIEL: He worries me. Plenty.

DANCING DAN: Forget him.

(MURIEL *pulls away.*)

MURIEL: I can't forget him. Heine came around today—

DANCING DAN: When is this?

MURIEL: This afternoon. Back at the club—looking for you. He scares me. It's all got me thinking again: we can't go on like this. We've gotta get out of this town.

DANCING DAN: Oh, we got plenty of time.

MURIEL: Dan, we don't. Besides, I can't keep high-kicking forever. (*Gestures at her costume*) I want more than this....And what about our dancing school?

DANCING DAN: I tell you what. After the New Year, we'll talk about it.

MURIEL: No. We've talked enough. You remember my girlfriend Kiki, in Frisco?

DANCING DAN: Sure. Grows up in my old neighborhood you tell me.

MURIEL: She wrote me. She's found a beautiful space that would be perfect for the school, and she wants us to come out and join her. I'd like more than anything to go out there with you, Dan. But if I have to, I'll go alone.

DANCING DAN: Let us not be hasty.

MURIEL: It's now or never. Kiki says the space won't stay open for long. This is our chance. I just feel it. And with everything that's happening, if we don't go now, I feel we might not get a second chance.

DANCING DAN: But what about Gammer O'Neill? You always say you cannot leave her.

MURIEL: I would never leave her. Gammer will come with us.

(GAMMER O'NEILL *appears, sitting in a chair draped with a stocking. She is holding a letter.*)

DANCING DAN: Come with us? Do you think she can make such a trip? She's so old. This could be her very last Christmas.

MURIEL: I know that.

DANCING DAN: She is probably hanging her Christmas stocking at this very moment.

GAMMER O'NEILL: Dear Santa, I have been particularly good this year.

MURIEL: Dan, I don't want to talk about Gammer right now.

DANCING DAN: Does she write her letter again?

GAMMER O'NEILL: And you always bring me such nice things.

MURIEL: Of course she did. She writes him every year.

GAMMER O'NEILL: The darning egg you bring me last year was certainly useful. And the Fels-Naptha soap the year before was nice too.

DANCING DAN: I never see anyone who loves Christmas so much.

MURIEL: Listen to me—

DANCING DAN: She is the sweetest thing.

MURIEL: Dan…

GAMMER O'NEILL: Still, I always hope that maybe once, just once, dear Santa, you could come through for me and fill my stocking with beautiful gifts. Something really sparkly? What do you say?

DANCING DAN: You are telling me just the other night how you wish you can give Gammer O'Neill one real big Christmas before the old doll puts her checks back in the rack.

MURIEL: I did buy Gammer a few extra gifts this year. Only I can't afford much….

DANCING DAN: I know, sweetheart. You always do right by her.

GAMMER O'NEILL: I'm counting on ya, Santa. Could ya come through? I still believe in you, honey. Yours in hope, Gammer O'Neill.

(Lights fade on GAMMER O'NEILL.)

MURIEL: She means the world to me, Dan.

(DANCING DAN pulls MURIEL close.)

DANCING DAN: To both of us. And we will stay right here for her.

(BLONDY bursts in.)

BLONDY: Here you are! I am sorry to break in on your little teet a teet. But we need to leave right now. Heine Schmitz is at the party.

DANCING DAN: I know. I see him cooling his heels in the front hall.

BLONDY: Goodbye, Muriel.

DANCING DAN: But I am not leaving. This is a swell party. I am not afraid of Heine.

(Enter HEINE.)

HEINE: Hello, Dancing Dan. *(He pulls out a gun.)*

DANCING DAN: Hello, Heine. What brings you here?

HEINE: I see Santa Claus dancing with some very large doll. And I say to myself, "There is only one guy with fancy footwork like this."

DANCING DAN: For such a hefty doll, that Wilberforce dame has a lot of rhythm.

HEINE: Let us take a walk, Dancing Dan.

(BITSY enters. HEINE quickly hides his gun.)

BITSY: Santa! There you are. My guests are asking for you. *(To* HEINE *and* MURIEL*)* What are you two doing back here?

(THE DUTCHMAN *enters, followed by* MYRTON.*)*

THE DUTCHMAN: *(Holding up keys)* We got a car! *(Seeing* BITSY, HEINE, *and the others)* Oh. Hello, Heine.

BITSY: Heine? Who's Heine?

DANCING DAN: Mrs Albright, have you not met Mr Heine Schmitz?

BITSY: *(Shocked)* You're Heine Schmitz?

HEINE: I am.

BITSY: This is indeed a great pleasure! I have heard so much about you from my dear friend Judge Thrasher.

HEINE: The pleasure is mine.

BITSY: You're too kind.

HEINE: I have a small task to complete, but perhaps when I return we can continue our conversation.

BITSY: I admire your dedication to business. It does surprise me, however, that you make your own deliveries. I was led to believe that you have something of an empire.

DANCING DAN: Why, this is the very word I use when talking about Heine Schmitz. He builds himself an empire from the island of Manhattan to the borough of Brooklyn and even all the way to New Jersey.

BLONDY: Let us not forget the Bronx and Staten Island.

DANCING DAN: We must never forget the Bronx and Staten Island. As far as the eye can see, you will see the enterprises of this man.

THE DUTCHMAN: A most industrious citizen.

DANCING DAN: Heine, you have, what, four hundred guys working for you?

HEINE: Five hundred. Let's go, Dancing Dan.

BITSY: Five hundred employees. That is impressive, Mr Schmitz. I know what it takes to manage a business of that size.

DANCING DAN: Exactly. Attention to detail. This is Heine Schmitz. Mrs Albright, for a customer as respected as yourself, he will even personally deliver beer—

HEINE: Champagne.

DANCING DAN: And champagne to your doorstep. All this he learns from the time he is…well, the age of one of those young boys out there.

THE DUTCHMAN: Yes, one of those boys could have been Heine Schmitz many years ago.

DANCING DAN: A boy alone in the world, trying to make good.

BLONDY: Pulling himself up by his bootstraps…

THE DUTCHMAN: Climbing the ladder of success…

DANCING DAN: Step by step on the shoulders of other men. And now he sits on top of the world, looking out over…his empire.

(The guys, joined by MURIEL and MYRTON, applaud HEINE.)

BITSY: I am sure these accolades are well deserved, Mr Schmitz.

HEINE: Call me Heine.

BITSY: And please call me Bitsy.

HEINE: Thank you, Bitsy.

BITSY: When I came in I could see that you were in conference with...Dancing Dan is it?

DANCING DAN: Yes, ma'am.

BITSY: Now I understand that for reasons best known to yourself, Heine, you may need to eliminate Dancing Dan. And perhaps his friends. This is entirely your affair, and I won't interfere.

HEINE: You are a most understanding woman, Bitsy. *(He pulls out his gun again.)*

BITSY: All I ask is that you not get blood on my Feraghan Sarouk carpet.

HEINE: It is a beautiful carpet.

BITSY: It is, isn't it? Persian.

(As one, the guys step onto the carpet.)

HEINE: You have nothing to worry about, Bitsy. Dancing Dan and I will be leaving.

(HEINE nudges DANCING DAN forward with the barrel of his pistol. MURIEL gasps.)

BITSY: There is, however, another possibility.

DANCING DAN: Let us hear this other possibility, Heine.

BITSY: If you would rather not spend a tiresome evening dealing with the police and feeling all that warmth.

(The guys and HEINE look at each other, confused.)

MURIEL: *(Helpfully)* Heat?

BITSY: Heat. Exactly. You might prefer instead to come back into the party with me. There are quite a few important and highly influential guests I would like you to meet. Do you know Senator Prye?

HEINE: Only what I read in the papers.

BITSY: Don't believe everything you read. He could be most helpful to a man of your position. Most helpful. *(To* DANCING DAN*)* I also want you to come back to the party. *(To* HEINE*)* You see, this is an important night for me. I am building a new wing at the Whitley School for Wayward Boys, and Judy Wilberforce is on the verge of writing a substantial check. And I owe this to you, Dancing Dan. Judy tells me that dancing with you is more intoxicating than champagne. Though your champagne is very good, Heine.

HEINE: As I promised, Bitsy. *(He pockets his gun and moves discreetly to a desk.)*

DANCING DAN: This is indeed a high-class party, Mrs Albright. I enjoy myself every minute. But the sad time has come when I and my friends must leave. The boys have their gifts from Santa and all is well.

MYRTON: Yes, the children are once more settled in the library, Madam.

THE DUTCHMAN: As a father of eight, I know wherefore I speak, and I can tell you that Myrton knows his business when it comes to boys that will be boys. He sees how much the youngsters enjoy their eggnog, and he brings them all back for more of that good Christmas cheer.

BITSY: Yes, Myrton, I must say you have done your job well this evening. You will find a healthy bonus in your Christmas stocking.

MYRTON: Thank you, Madam. You are most generous.

DANCING DAN: Muriel, if I am not mistaken, it is almost time for the Moonbeams to perform.

MURIEL: We are on in five.

DANCING DAN: Then may I suggest, Mrs Albright, that the girls can handle it from here. On with the show!

BITSY: *(To* MURIEL*)* Yes, it must start on time. Please go get ready.

MURIEL: Merry Christmas to all! *(She hurries to the door, blows* DANCING DAN *a kiss, and exits.)*

BITSY: Would you at least, for me, Dancing Dan, give Mrs Wilberforce one last spin around the floor?

HEINE: Forget Mrs Wilberforce. *(Hands* BITSY *a check)* For your new wing.

*(*BITSY *is staggered by the amount.)*

BITSY: My goodness! Heine!

HEINE: Well, it is Christmas, ain't it?

BITSY: Yes, but this is quite unexpected—though very welcome, to be sure. You *must* join the party now. I simply won't take no for an answer.

HEINE: I'd be happy to, Bitsy.

THE DUTCHMAN: Well, isn't that nice. Everything is settled and we can be on our way.

DANCING DAN: We *do* need to get going.

HEINE: No you don't. *(Grabs* DANCING DAN *violently by the coat)* You are not going anywhere. You and me still have business to discuss. And if Mrs Albright wants you to dance, you will dance. You hear me!?

DANCING DAN: I hear you.

BITSY: Thank you, Heine. But first things first. Let me introduce you around.

*(*HEINE *releases* DANCING DAN*.)*

HEINE: Do not move a foot from this spot until I say so. Or you—*and* your two pals here—will be sorry. Very sorry.

*(*BITSY *slips her arm around* HEINE'S *arm and leads him to the door.)*

BITSY: Tell me, Heine. Have you any political aspirations? We happen to be looking for someone to run for governor.

HEINE: Izzat so?

BITSY: Oh, yes. Go on in, and we'll talk. I need a brief word with the butler.

(HEINE *goes.* BITSY *turns to* MYRTON.)

BITSY: *(Indicating the guys)* You can get rid of them now.

MYRTON: Very good, Madam.

(BITSY *goes off after* HEINE.)

(MYRTON *shuts the door. The guys look at each other. They can't believe their luck.* DANCING DAN *starts yanking off his Santa costume.*)

DANCING DAN: The way I see it, if we drive as fast as Myrton, we'll hit P A in two hours.

BLONDY: By my watch, an hour and fifty.

THE DUTCHMAN: Myrton, you going to be all right?

MYRTON: You have a clear night for traveling.

(DANCING DAN *clutches the wrapped package he used for padding and gestures to the Santa costume on the floor.*)

DANCING DAN: The suit is all yours, Myrton. Save it for next Christmas.

MYRTON: Thank you. *(To* THE DUTCHMAN*)* But who knows what next year will bring.

THE DUTCHMAN: New friends and sunnier climes.

(*They are heading for the door...*)

BLONDY: Wait! What about the car?

MYRTON: Mr Dutchman has the keys. But of course I know nothing of the car you are about to steal without my knowledge.

BLONDY: Of course.

THE DUTCHMAN: See ya, Myrton. Start packing.

(As they go:)

DANCING DAN: Remember, I still have one quick errand to run back in Manhattan. It will not take long. I will be in and out!

(They exit.)

MYRTON: Cheerio!

(Lights)

(THE DUTCHMAN is at the wheel of a Studebaker on the road to P A. DANCING DAN is in the passenger seat. BLONDY sits in the back. The guys are finishing up a rendition of "Ain't We Got Fun?")

ALL:
In the winter, in the summer,
Don't we have fun?
Times are bum and getting bummer,
Still we have fun.
There's nothing surer,
The rich get rich and the poor get children,
In the meantime, in between time,
Ain't we got fun?

BLONDY: Another round?

(BLONDY pours whiskey into a paper cup. He pours remarkably well, considering that the car is clearly moving at a high speed. He hands a cup to DANCING DAN, who offers it to THE DUTCHMAN.)

DANCING DAN: Dutchman?

THE DUTCHMAN: *(Taking the cup)* Thank you. I will have just one more. I am driving, after all.

(BLONDY hands a second cup to DANCING DAN.)

DANCING DAN: Here is to Heine Schmitz. I hope he does not miss us too much.

ALL: To Heine!

(They drink.)

DANCING DAN: Besides hot Tom and Jerry, I think rock candy and rye whiskey is the best drink for Christmas Eve.

BLONDY: I just wish we buy more rock candy.

THE DUTCHMAN: Well, rock candy and rye whiskey without the rock candy is still not a bad drink.

BLONDY: If only Dixie's Drugstore does not run out of rock candy. We could go down the block to Dillmore's, but you are back too quick, Dancing Dan.

DANCING DAN: What do I tell you: just one quick errand. In and out, and… *(Snaps his fingers)* it is done!

BLONDY: How much longer, Dutchman?

THE DUTCHMAN: Not long now.

BLONDY: Good. Because we are almost out of rye whiskey.

DANCING DAN: Why do you not buy more of this second ingredient?

BLONDY: We buy it from Dixie for medicinal purposes.

THE DUTCHMAN: Doc Moggs writes the prescription for me last year. For my rheumatism. In case I ever happen to get any rheumatism.

BLONDY: Dixie says we can only buy two bottles at a time on the prescription. But I never hear this rule before.

THE DUTCHMAN: I think this is a Christmas Eve rule, because on Christmas Eve Dixie runs a high-stakes card game in the back, and it is attended by many thirsty players who will be disappointed if they cannot quench their thirst, and they are not such citizens as Dixie wants to disappoint.

(There is a pause. BLONDY *and* DANCING DAN *look out the car windows. It starts to snow.)*

DANCING DAN: You know, seeing these little villages all lit up for Christmas and the holly wreaths on the doors...

BLONDY: Are we anywhere near Akron?

DANCING DAN: Somehow it makes me think of holidays back in Frisco. My old man would set up a tree in the front parlor, and all the girls would sing carols around Skinny Weller's piano.

BLONDY: I know what you mean. I get a little homesick, too. Of course, even if I am home, the chances are I will not be seeing any Christmas trees. *(He drinks.)*

(THE DUTCHMAN *makes a sudden turn. The guys all lurch to the side. It becomes apparent that the car is speeding over a bumpy road.)*

DANCING DAN: Are you sure you know where you are going? This appears to be an untraveled road.

THE DUTCHMAN: I know I am on the right road. I am following the big star you see up ahead.

BLONDY: *(Peering out the window)* I do not see a star.

THE DUTCHMAN: I remember seeing this star always in front of me when I am going along this road before.

DANCING DAN: When are you on this road before?

BLONDY: Where is this star?

THE DUTCHMAN: Oh, I am on this road some eight or nine months ago. On the night of the heist.

BLONDY & DANCING DAN: The heist!?

THE DUTCHMAN: Well, you see, here is the thing. About eight or nine months ago I am mobbed up with Jimmy

Bates, a very classy, heavy guy, and we make quite a good thing going around knocking off safes in small-town jugs and post offices.

DANCING DAN: This is once quite a popular custom in this country.

BLONDY: And so the two of you are on this road...

THE DUTCHMAN: Yes. A party Jimmy knows gives him a tip about a big payroll in a safe at a factory, and we come here to Pennsylvania. About nine months ago...

(A shadow play. The silhouettes of two men appear. Above them shines a bright star. The silhouettes follow the star, which ends up shining over a large safe.)

(The Dutchman silhouette goes to work on the lock while the Jimmy silhouette stands guard.)

THE DUTCHMAN: The safe is one of the new kind. The factory is up to date, and they do okay. This new brand of safe is a lot of bother. But I do not mind the bother. And so for I and Jimmy it is a very prosperous business.

(The silhouette of the safe explodes, and cash flies.)

THE DUTCHMAN: The payroll amounts to maybe fifty Gs, and I and Jimmy are thinking this is the easiest money we make yet.

(The silhouette of a bookkeeper appears. He is wearing the green visor of his profession. He leads in the silhouettes of two cops, who wield guns.)

THE DUTCHMAN: Then a nosy office guy and the gendarmes butt in, and they wish to speak with us.

(The silhouettes of two cops rush forward. A tussle ensues. Shots ring out. The Jimmy silhouette falls.)

THE DUTCHMAN: It does not go well. What with one thing and another, Jimmy is cooled off. *(He chokes up for a moment, then goes on.)* I manage to get away, but I am shot up some, and it is not easy moving across the countryside.

(The star once more appears in the night sky. The Dutchman silhouette, clutching the gripsack, stumbles along, following the star.)

THE DUTCHMAN: Fifty Gs in a gripsack is a very heavy load, and there is no chance I can keep lugging it around. So I come to an old deserted barn, and I hide the gripsack where no curious passerby will find it.

(A barn appears on the horizon, just below the star, and The Dutchman silhouette moves toward the building.)

THE DUTCHMAN: In the meantime, I make my way to New Brunswick and lay up at my uncle's place until my wounds heal. This takes considerable time, as I cannot take it nowadays the way I can when I am younger.

(The image of the barn fades, leaving only the star shining in the sky.)

THE DUTCHMAN: I figure to go back one day and pick up the bag with all the money. But every time I think about going back to the old barn, I run out of confidence. And though I need this dough most bad, I cannot get myself to head back to P A alone. This is what happens when you commence to get old. So I figure it might be a good idea to bring somebody else in to help me, and I am still figuring this when we all meet up at Good Time Charley's and Heine walks in.

(This information sinks in.)

DANCING DAN: So, you are taking us to this old barn now.

BLONDY: Where you have hidden the dough.

(THE DUTCHMAN nods.)

DANCING DAN: What is your proposition, Dutchman?

THE DUTCHMAN: Well, I am willing to make an even split three ways.

DANCING DAN: One-third of fifty Gs is by no means pretzels in these times. I will gladly assist you in this enterprise.

BLONDY: Yes. This appeals to me as a legitimate proposition, because there is no doubt this dough is coming to you, and from now on I am strictly legit.

THE DUTCHMAN: Let us seal the matter with one final drink of rock candy and rye whiskey without the rock candy.

(BLONDY *pours the last of the whiskey into their cups.*)

(*At the same time:*)

BLONDY: Skoal!

DANCING DAN: Cheers!

THE DUTCHMAN: Mud in your eye!

(*They down their drinks.*)

BLONDY: Hey! Now I see the star.

DANCING DAN: No, that is no star.

(*A barn comes into view through the falling snow. The star is actually a light shining through a window of the ramshackle building.* THE DUTCHMAN *brings the car to a stop.*)

THE DUTCHMAN: Well, this looks very much like my old barn. But my barn does not call for a light in it.

DANCING DAN: Let us investigate this matter.

(*The three guys climb out of the car and approach the rickety barn. They all peer through the lighted window.*)

BLONDY: Who is that doll?

DANCING DAN: Does she live here?

THE DUTCHMAN: There was no doll living here before.

BLONDY: If she does, she certainly knows about the money and the gripsack.

THE DUTCHMAN: There was nobody here.

DANCING DAN: If she finds fifty Gs, I do not think she will still be living in a barn.

BLONDY: This appears to be a very sick doll.

THE DUTCHMAN: Listen, the chances are that her ever-loving husband, or someone, is in town or maybe over to the nearest neighbors digging up assistance and will be back in a jiffy. I propose we lay low and wait to see what happens.

BLONDY: You can see from the snow that no one has been in or out of this barn for a good long time. And only a bounder and a cad will walk away from a sick doll, especially a sick doll who is a total stranger to him. In fact, it will take a very large heel to do such a thing. The idea is for us to see if we can do anything for this sick doll.

DANCING DAN: I will go in with you, Blondy.

(They look to THE DUTCHMAN.*)*

THE DUTCHMAN: Let us all go in.

*(*DANCING DAN *and* THE DUTCHMAN *follow* BLONDY *into the barn.)*

(The interior of the long-neglected barn is lit by a dim lantern hanging on a post. The place is furnished with a table and chairs and a tin stove, in which there is a low fire. Across the room is a makeshift bed, next to which is a manger. In the bed is a woman.)

(As BLONDY, THE DUTCHMAN, *and* DANCING DAN *enter, the woman half raises up to look at the guys.)*

CLARABELLE: Blondy Swanson!?

BLONDY: Miss Clarabelle Cobb!?

(BLONDY *stares in stupefied silence.* CLARABELLE *groans in pain. The guys go to her.* THE DUTCHMAN *bends down and looks closely at a very pregnant* CLARABELLE.)

THE DUTCHMAN: This is more than a sick doll.

BLONDY: *(Still in a daze)* This is Miss Clarabelle Cobb.

THE DUTCHMAN: Well, we have quite a delicate situation here. I must request you guys to step outside.

BLONDY: This is Miss Clarabelle Cobb.

THE DUTCHMAN: What we really need for this case is a doctor, but it is too late to send for one. I will endeavor to do the best I can under the circumstances. *(He takes off his overcoat.)*

DANCING DAN: Come on, Blondy. Let us do as The Dutchman says.

BLONDY: This is Miss Clarabelle Cobb.

THE DUTCHMAN: Do not worry about anything, Blondy. *(To* CLARABELLE*)* You will be just fine, Miss. I am maybe a little out of practice since my old lady puts her checks back in the rack, but she leaves eight kids alive and kicking, and I bring them all in except one, because we are seldom able to afford a croaker.

(DANCING DAN *leads* BLONDY *out of the barn as* THE DUTCHMAN *tends to* CLARABELLE.)

(*Outside the barn,* DANCING DAN *and* BLONDY *wait in the cold. They are silent for a moment.*)

DANCING DAN: So, you okay?

BLONDY: I hear Miss Clarabelle Cobb gets married to a legitimate guy, and what I want to know is where is this legitimate guy right now?

DANCING DAN: I wish I knew. I myself would give him a piece of my mind.

BLONDY: If Miss Clarabelle Cobb were my ever-loving wife, I would not be absent at a time like this.

DANCING DAN: Well, you are here now.

BLONDY: Dancing Dan...I never tell anybody this, but six years ago this very night I make a big mistake. The biggest mistake of my life.

DANCING DAN: Yes, a night like this gets you thinking....You believe in miracles? Well, second chances.

BLONDY: What do you mean?

DANCING DAN: I mean look at me. If I do not put on that Santa suit back at Good Time Charley's, I would be very dead right now. But here I am, alive and kicking. And here is this new little baby waiting to get born. And here is Miss Clarabelle Cobb, and here you are...

BLONDY: Yeah?...

DANCING DAN: Well...it gets you thinking.

BLONDY: You know what I am thinking?

DANCING DAN: What?

BLONDY: I am thinking I am going to take care of this little baby that is getting itself born.

DANCING DAN: This is a very noble gesture, Blondy.

BLONDY: I will watch over this baby. I will be like a godfather to her and see that she gets a proper start in this life. It is a night for second chances.

DANCING DAN: And you know what it is got me thinking?

BLONDY: What?

DANCING DAN: I am thinking what it would be like to have a little nipper of my own—a girl that looks like Miss Muriel O'Neill or a boy that looks like me.

BLONDY: One thing sure, your kid will be a good dancer. *(Pause)* And Miss Clarabelle Cobb's little girl will be a beauty. Like her mom.

(From inside the barn, a baby cries. THE DUTCHMAN's voice calls out.)

THE DUTCHMAN: *(Off)* Blondy! Dancing Dan!

(BLONDY and DANCING DAN hurry back into the barn.)

(Inside, the fire in the stove is now blazing cheerfully. CLARABELLE, covered by THE DUTCHMAN's overcoat, lies quietly, smiling up at the guys.)

(THE DUTCHMAN proudly pulls back an edge of the overcoat to reveal a baby cradled in CLARABELLE's arms.)

THE DUTCHMAN: It is a boy.

BLONDY: A boy?!

CLARABELLE: Yes, Blondy, a very healthy boy.

THE DUTCHMAN: A real darberoo.

DANCING DAN: This baby is a great credit to you in every respect, Dutchman.

THE DUTCHMAN: Furthermore, the mamma is doing as well as can be expected. She is as strong a doll as ever I see.

CLARABELLE: Oh, thank you.

DANCING DAN: When we go through town we will send back a croaker just to make sure there are no complications.

THE DUTCHMAN: Yes, but I guarantee the croaker will not have much to do.

(DANCING DAN motions to THE DUTCHMAN, and they move discreetly away.)

(THE DUTCHMAN *leads* DANCING DAN *to a corner of the barn, where they kneel down and busy themselves with the floorboards.*)

(BLONDY *pulls a chair over beside* CLARABELLE'*s bed.*)

CLARABELLE: I don't suppose I should even ask what you are doing here, Blondy.

BLONDY: I cannot blame you for thinking the worst, but the honest truth is I am here to help a friend on a legitimate business enterprise. I put the old days behind me.

CLARABELLE: I never thought I would see you again, Blondy.

BLONDY: After you take a run-out—after you go back to Akron, Ohio, I promise myself I will pack up hauling wet goods and look you up and marry you.

CLARABELLE: I was waiting, Blondy, and hoping. I waited a long time.

BLONDY: I keep putting it off and putting it off. And then one day I hear you marry a legitimate guy in Akron, Ohio.

CLARABELLE: Yes. Joseph Hatcher. (*Holds back a sob*) You would like him.

BLONDY: If he treats you wrong, I will not like him much.

CLARABELLE: Oh, no, he's very good to me. Of course, he never tried to give me presents like diamond bracelets and fur coats.

BLONDY: You never accept one gift from me.

CLARABELLE: I enjoyed all the flowers and the candy. But I couldn't keep those other things. No nice girl could. You know when I returned that sable coat that very cold day, the girls in the dressing room said there is a limit even to eccentricity.

BLONDY: You was always a nice girl. From the day I hear you are married, I never look at another doll. Or anyway, not much.

CLARABELLE: I'm sorry I left without saying goodbye in person.

BLONDY: Well, I got your letter. Who knows, it could be you do the right thing. But why is your ever-loving husband not here? Where is this Joseph Hatcher anyhow?

(DANCING DAN *and* THE DUTCHMAN, *holding a gripsack, rejoin* BLONDY *at* CLARABELLE's *bedside.*)

CLARABELLE: *(With a sob)* Oh, Blondy, my Joseph is in big trouble!

BLONDY: What does he pull?

CLARABELLE: No, he did not do anything. That's the trouble. You see, my Joseph is a bookkeeper, and we were so happy in Akron, and then his firm sent him out here to Pennsylvania, and now he's in jail, but he didn't do anything.

BLONDY: He is framed?

CLARABELLE: Yes! His trial is coming up, and they say it is an open-and-shut case, but it is all a lie! I've tried everything to get him out. I spent every dime of our money, and I had to move out of our house.

BLONDY: How do you end up here?

CLARABELLE: Doc Kelton—he took good care of us when we were sick last year—is letting me stay here. This is his barn. He has a wife and three children. There's no room in the house.

BLONDY: Tell me what happens with Joseph Hatcher.

CLARABELLE: Oh, it's a terrible story. I don't know how we'll ever recover. It all happened one night about nine months ago. My Joseph is working late in his office—

he's a very dedicated worker. That's why they brought him out here.

(We again see that fateful star shining in the heavens. The silhouette of a bookkeeper, Joseph Hatcher, appears, working an adding machine at his desk.)

CLARABELLE: He thinks he's the only one in the factory, but he hears voices in the next room and goes to investigate.

(Joseph's silhouette enters the room and discovers the silhouettes of The Dutchman and his partner Jimmy.)

CLARABELLE: He sees two robbers! He tries to stop them, but they hit him on the head and tie him up in his office.

(Joseph's silhouette is now tied to a chair.)

CLARABELLE: The factory has a brand-new safe, and when my Joseph comes to, he hears the robbers blow it up.

(KABOOM! The silhouette of the safe explodes, and cash flies.)

CLARABELLE: Even though he's tied up, he struggles to break his bonds.

(Joseph's silhouette twists and turns in his chair and frees himself.)

CLARABELLE: My Joseph is very athletic. You would not think it to look at him. It is surprising in a bookkeeper. He manages to get free and calls the police.

(Joseph's silhouette grabs the phone.)

CLARABELLE: They arrive just in time. One of the robbers gets shot, but the other one gets away with the money. And they never find him.

(The Jimmy silhouette is shot and killed. The Dutchman silhouette runs off with the gripsack full of money.)

CLARABELLE: My Joseph should be a hero for putting his life in danger and trying to save the day, but instead he's in jail.

(The silhouette of a cop holds a gun on Joseph's silhouette.)

CLARABELLE: And it's all because the factory foreman, a man by the name of Ambersham, starts spreading a rotten lie about my Joseph.

(Lights reveal AMBERSHAM, *giving a statement to the police.)*

AMBERSHAM: Oh, yes, Joseph Hatcher had to have been in on it. I'm telling you this was an inside job. How else could these hoodlums have known about the payroll in the safe? Pretending to get knocked out and tied up and then calling the police was all part of Hatcher's plan. See what I mean? What do we really know about this man? He's a stranger here. He's not one of us. He's from Ohio. It was just bad luck for Hatcher that the robbers were a mite too slow and were still in the room when our town's fine officers of the law arrived. He won't get his share of the loot now. But I hope and pray that he will receive the full weight of the justice he so richly deserves. My full name? Arnold Spencer Ambersham, factory foreman.

(Lights fade on AMBERSHAM.*)*

CLARABELLE: And now my Joseph is behind bars, awaiting trial, and everybody thinks he's guilty, and they all say the judge will throw the book at him.

*(*DOC KELTON, *a kindly but no-nonsense country doctor in his fifties, enters.)*

DOC KELTON: Hey, what is all this? Who are you guys?

CLARABELLE: It's all right, Doc…

DOC KELTON: Get out of my barn!

DANCING DAN: Hold your horses, pal.

BLONDY: You're the doc?

DOC KELTON: Yes, I'm her doctor and this is my barn. Clarabelle, are you all right?

CLARABELLE: Yes, we're fine. Everything's just fine. This is an old friend of mine.

BLONDY: Blondy Swanson.

(BLONDY *extends his hand.* DOC KELTON *ignores it.*)

DOC KELTON: What is he doing here?

THE DUTCHMAN: Everything is A-O K, Doc. See, I have eight of my own, and—

CLARABELLE: It's a boy. Look!

DOC KELTON: Give us some privacy, fellas.

(THE DUTCHMAN *and* DANCING DAN *take* BLONDY *to a corner of the barn and open the gripsack.*)

THE DUTCHMAN: It is all here.

DANCING DAN: Fifty Gs in small lovely banknotes.

(BLONDY *takes the gripsack.*)

BLONDY: From what Miss Clarabelle Cobb says, her Joseph puts up no little struggle for this sugar.

THE DUTCHMAN: Yes, he is without a doubt the very same young guy we are compelled to truss up. As I recollect it, he wishes to battle for his employer's dough, and I personally tap him over the coco with a blackjack. I do not know, of course, that he is the ever-loving husband of Miss Clarabelle Cobb. I am sorry for that, Blondy.

BLONDY: Well, he interferes with your business. He gives you no choice.

THE DUTCHMAN: Also, he is by no means the guy who tips us off about the dough in the safe. As I remember it now, it is nobody but the guy whose name Miss

Clarabelle Cobb mentions. It is this guy Ambersham, the foreman of the joint.

(DOC KELTON, *carrying his medical bag, steps over to the guys.*)

DOC KELTON: Well, everything seems to be satisfactory.

DANCING DAN: Say it to The Dutchman.

THE DUTCHMAN: It all comes back to me.

DOC KELTON: Mother and child are just fine.

BLONDY: This is good news.

DOC KELTON: But they need to rest.

THE DUTCHMAN: Sure, they must rest now. I have eight of my own, and I delivered all but one, because we could usually not afford a croaker.

BLONDY: *(To* DANCING DAN *and* THE DUTCHMAN*)* Let me speak with the doc for a minute. *(To* DOC KELTON*)* Can I have a word with you?

DOC KELTON: What's this about?

(BLONDY *and* DOC KELTON *go off to the side, while* DANCING DAN *and* THE DUTCHMAN *go over to* CLARABELLE.*)

THE DUTCHMAN: Well, Miss Clarabelle, you are in good hands now.

DANCING DAN: It is nice seeing you again.

CLARABELLE: Oh, nice to see you too.

DANCING DAN: I always enjoy watching you dance in the Georgie White Scandals.

CLARABELLE: That was a long time ago. Things happen, don't they?

DANCING DAN: *(Agreeing)* Things change. But anyway, Miss Muriel O'Neill also sees you dance, and she always says you have a large talent.

CLARABELLE: No, I never did.... But it's sweet of you to say so.

THE DUTCHMAN: I would like to ask you, is Joseph Hatcher recovered from any injuries on the night in question?

CLARABELLE: He received a bad bump on his head, but it could have been much worse.

THE DUTCHMAN: Yes, it is lucky whoever conked him had no aim to do more harm.

CLARABELLE: Anyhow, the problem is not the bump on his head. The problem is...oh, my poor Joseph!.... *(She weeps.)*

*(*BLONDY *and* DOC KELTON *rejoin the group.)*

DOC KELTON: Now, young lady, we won't have any of that. You just dry those eyes. We need to think about this new little boy here. You were certainly lucky these fellows showed up when they did.

CLARABELLE: I know. They're my saviors!

DANCING DAN: Well, I wouldn't say that.

THE DUTCHMAN: More like elves.

BLONDY: Yes, metaphoric elves.

DOC KELTON: Whatever you say. *(To* CLARABELLE*)* We're going to get this boy's father back home just as soon as we can.

CLARABELLE: Will you, Doc? Can you?

DOC KELTON: I now have some information that I believe my good friend Captain McCarthy will find extremely interesting. I think I can promise you we'll have Joseph out of prison within twenty-four hours.

CLARABELLE: Oh, Doc, thank you. It's a miracle!

DANCING DAN: Or a second chance anyhow.

DOC KELTON: *(To the guys)* The thing is, Captain McCarthy isn't what you'd call an early riser—and certainly not on Christmas day. It will be three or four hours at least before I can speak to him. Plenty of time to, let us say, get to New Jersey. I hope you gents have a safe and speedy journey.

DANCING DAN: Yes, we will be on our way now, Doc. So long.

THE DUTCHMAN: Thanks.

DANCING DAN: *(To* BLONDY*)* We will see you outside.

*(*DANCING DAN *and* THE DUTCHMAN *exit.)*

DOC KELTON: *(To* CLARABELLE*)* And I'll be right back with Mrs Kelton. She'll bring you a breakfast you won't soon forget. She's not so crazy about kids, but she just loves newborns. *(He exits.)*

*(*CLARABELLE *looks at* BLONDY *and holds the baby up to him. He tentatively takes the baby, cradles him, and then tenderly kisses his forehead.)*

*(*BLONDY *hands the baby back to* CLARABELLE*.)*

CLARABELLE: I will name him for you, Blondy. By the way, what is your right name?

BLONDY: Olaf.

CLARABELLE: *(Beat)* I will still name him for you.

BLONDY: Goodbye, Miss Clarabelle.

CLARABELLE: Merry Christmas, Blondy.

*(*BLONDY *exits with the gripsack tucked under his arm.)*

(Lights fade on the barn.)

(Inside the Studebaker, THE DUTCHMAN *is again at the wheel,* DANCING DAN *beside him,* BLONDY *in the back seat. The car is once again moving at a high speed. Outside, dawn is breaking.)*

THE DUTCHMAN: I am thinking about this Ambersham, and here is what I think. He is supposed to get his bit of dough for his trouble on that night at the factory. I do not approve of his conduct toward Joseph Hatcher, but it is only fair that I carry out this agreement as the executor of the estate of my late comrade. I will take Ambersham's cut from the top, and we will split the remainder. But it will still leave us with plenty of potatoes in the gripsack.

BLONDY: Well, Dutchman, I tell you…

(*A police siren wails behind them.*)

DANCING DAN: Now what?

BLONDY: What a night! Better pull over.

THE DUTCHMAN: You are not serious!

BLONDY: Pull over!

(THE DUTCHMAN *brings the car to a stop.*)

(*A* COP *approaches the car.*)

COP: Where's the fire, boys? (*Peers inside the car*) This is a very fine car. What are you guys carrying in this fine car, anyway? What's in that gripsack?

(BLONDY *hands him the gripsack. The* COP *opens it.*)

COP: Well, well, well… (*He pulls an empty bottle from what is clearly an empty gripsack.*) I know what is formerly in this bottle.

THE DUTCHMAN: This what?

COP: This bottle!

DANCING DAN: I tell you the truth when I say the bottle is formerly full of medicine.

COP: Oh, wise guys, eh? Three wise guys. Trying to kid somebody, eh? I have a good mind to take you in and hold you on suspicion. But…it's Christmas Day. So I will be Santa Claus to you and let you go ahead…wise guys. *(He tosses the gripsack into the car and walks away.)*

(THE DUTCHMAN and DANCING DAN turn to face BLONDY.)

BLONDY: This Doc Kelton strikes me as a right guy in every respect. So I leave the money with him to be returned to its rightful owners and to help clear the name of Joseph Hatcher. *(Patting his breast pocket)* But I hold back two Gs for you, Dutchman. To make good on your marker to Little Gringo.

(THE DUTCHMAN resumes driving.)

THE DUTCHMAN: Wise guys. Yes, this is what we are, to be sure. We are wise guys. If we are not wise guys, we will still have the gripsack full of fifty Gs for the copper to find. And if the copper finds the gripsack full of fifty Gs, he will wish to take us to the jailhouse for investigation, and if he wishes to take us there, I fear we will be in plenty of heat about now. And personally, I am sick and tired of heat.

DANCING DAN: So what now, Dutchman?

THE DUTCHMAN: Well, I make plans to head down to Florida with Myrton. After I pay off Little Gringo, I will be ready to try Myrton's surefire system at Hialeah.

(MYRTON appears in his room at the Long Island mansion. He is opening up a Christmas card.)

MYRTON: From Mrs Albright… *(He pulls out a bundle of cash—his Christmas bonus—and kisses the money. He lifts a glass.)* To Hialeah! *(He starts packing a bag with summer clothes, singing a snippet of* Will You Love Me in December As You Do in May?*)*

(Lights)

THE DUTCHMAN: What about you, Dancing Dan?

DANCING DAN: Well, I tell you, what with one thing and another, this looks like a good time to go straight....

(In a bedroom of the Long Island mansion, BITSY and HEINE are in bed, drinking champagne.)

HEINE: I just do not like a guy pulling a fast one on me, that's all.

BITSY: Let me ask you this: if the jewels from Shapiro's Fine Jewelry never turn up, you save the ten-thousand-dollar-no-questions-asked reward, right?

HEINE: Right.

BITSY: And the jewels are insured?

HEINE: Yeah.

BITSY: Does your brother-in-law have anything to worry about?

HEINE: No.

BITSY: Does your sister have anything to worry about?

HEINE: No.

BITSY: So you have nothing to worry about.

HEINE: I just do not like a guy—

BITSY: Forget about Dancing Dan. He is small potatoes. You have an impressive future ahead of you, Heine. If you want to knock someone off, I'm sure we can think of a more suitable person.

(BITSY leans over and whispers in HEINE's ear. A smile crosses his face. They toast to the possibilities. Then they kiss passionately.)

(Lights)

BLONDY: Yes, get out while you are still young and you have your ever-loving.

DANCING DAN: I and Miss Muriel O'Neill will make a fresh start with a classy dancing school in San Francisco.

THE DUTCHMAN: San Fran?

DANCING DAN: Yessir, Frisco is waiting. I know the town. A dancing school with the two of us will be a sensation. The way I see it, it is now or never.

BLONDY: Let me propose a toast or two, even if we have no more rock candy and rye whiskey with which to toast. To Dancing Dan and his Muriel O'Neill and their new high-class dancing school on western shores.

BLONDY & THE DUTCHMAN: To Dancing Dan!

BLONDY: To the Dutchman and his new life in sunnier climes.

BLONDY & DANCING DAN: To The Dutchman!

BLONDY: To my dear Miss Clarabelle Cobb and sweet little baby Olaf.

(DANCING DAN *and* THE DUTCHMAN *react to the name.* BLONDY *nudges them.*)

DANCING DAN & THE DUTCHMAN: To baby Olaf!

BLONDY: And last of all to…what town are we in?

THE DUTCHMAN: I see the name on a sign back there. Bethlehem. Bethlehem, P A.

BLONDY: To Bethlehem, P A.

ALL: To Bethlehem!

(*Blackout*)

(*Lights up on the tiny Manhattan bedroom of* GAMMER O'NEILL. *Sunlight streams across a stocking hung on a chair at the foot of her bed. The stocking is filled with diamond necklaces and bracelets. On the chair itself is a sparkling pile of diamond brooches and rings. A couple of boxes are emblazoned with the name "SHAPIRO'S FINE JEWELRY". A diamond makes up the "o" in "Shapiro".)*

(GAMMER O'NEILL sits up, sees the overflowing stocking, and is awestruck by the wondrous diamond dazzle.)

GAMMER O'NEILL: Santa! Oh, honey! You come through!

(GAMMER O'NEILL grabs her heart, falls back on her pillow, and dies with joy in a blaze of white light.)

END OF PLAY

Glossary of Slang Terms

Bangle a bracelet or an anklet.

Bash a party.

Beezer the nose.

Blackjack a short, leather-covered club.

Blow to leave.

Blow-out a big party.

Bobs dollars.

Bootie a bootlegger.

Booting bootlegging.

Bottle and a bird A bottle of wine and a fine meal (pheasant, for example).

Bounder an ill-mannered, unscrupulous man.

Brawl a party.

Cad an unprincipled man.

Can a car.

Coco the head.

Collared arrested.

College prison.

Come through to do what is needed or anticipated.

Conk to hit.

Cooled off killed.

Cooling his heels waiting.

Copper a police officer.

Croaker a doctor.

Croaks dies.

Cut a share (of earnings or winnings).

Dame a woman.

Darberoo someone or something special, a beauty.

Doll a woman.

Dough money.

Framed to be falsely incriminated.

Front a legitimate cover for shady dealings.

G one thousand dollars.

Gee a guy.

Gendarmes police officers.

Go straight to become law-abiding.

Gripsack a small suitcase.

Guff nonsense.

Hauling wet goods transporting liquor.

Heat trouble, pressure.

Heavy imposing, tough.

Heel a contemptible, dishonorable man.

Heist a burglary.

Hold your horses calm down, restrain yourself.

Inside job a crime committed by, or with the help of, someone associated with the victim.

Jeeves a butler (from the character created by British humorist P G Wodehouse).

Joint a building, a place of business.

Jugs banks.

Knock off to rob.

Knock someone off to kill someone.

Loot stolen money.

Make a killing to get rich.

Marker a written promise to pay, an I O U.

Mobbed up partnered.

Noggin the head.

Old dolls' home a nursing home.

Potatoes money, dollars.

Pretzels a small amount of money.

Pull perpetrate (a crime or a fraud, for example).

Pulling a fast one committing a deceitful or treacherous act.

Put your checks back in the rack to die.

Racket a business or occupation.

Ritzy Fancy, elegant.

Run-out powder a sudden departure.

Second-story man a burglar who slips in through an upstairs window.

Shindig a festive party.

Slammer prison.

Slouch a lazy or inept person.

Small potatoes unimportant, inconsequential.

Sneezer prison.

Sugar money.

Swell wonderful.

Take plenty of outdoors on get away from.

Throw the book at to give a convicted criminal a harsh sentence.

Touting soliciting customers.

Welsh to default on a promise or a payment.

Wise guys smart alecks.